What you need to know —
about salvation

What you need to know —
about salvation

Peter Jeffery

 EVANGELICAL PRESS

EVANGELICAL PRESS
12 Wooler Street, Darlington, Co. Durham, DL1 1RQ, England

British Library Cataloguing in Publication Data available

ISBN 0 85234 347 7

Printed and bound in Great Britain by Cox & Wyman Ltd, Reading

Contents

God's way of salvation

Introduction

This book is written for the person who knows he or she is not a Christian but earnestly desires to become one. Such a desire is to be commended and encouraged, because it can sometimes be very frustrating. People often say, 'I know I am a sinner. I know Jesus is the only Saviour and I have asked him to save me, but nothing has happened.' There could be several reasons for this and one of the main ones would be a failure to truly understand the nature of salvation. By this I mean a failure to understand why salvation is so necessary and what salvation from sin involves.

It is because of this that the Bible insists that faith comes from hearing the Word of God (Romans 10:17). Desires and feelings are not enough. They need directing by the Scriptures, because almost everyone who seeks to find God starts off with preconceived notions. We all have ideas about God that are the product of half-truths and concepts that have not been thought through. Have you noticed how often people who have little or no Bible knowledge are very quick to make pronouncements about God, heaven and hell, sin and holiness? Words without knowledge can be dangerous, especially when they are words about God.

We are all entitled to our opinions about politics, music and a 101 different subjects, but opinions about God are worthless. On this subject we need the whole truth and nothing but the truth. From where can we get such infallible truth? The only source of truth about God is God himself. So faith, saving faith, comes as we hear what God has to say in his Word, the Bible.

To help you arrive at this truth here are twenty-one daily readings from the Bible. They are chosen for their importance in bringing to us the basic Bible message on salvation, and are arranged under three headings:

The God we have to deal with
Man's sin and need
God's way of salvation.

First of all, read the set passage for the day, praying that the Lord will speak to you through the Scriptures. Then read the explanation of the passage, and finally pray again that your heart, mind and will may receive God's truths.

The God we have to deal with

Faith comes from hearing

The apostle Paul, who wrote these words, had a deep concern for his fellow Israelites. He wanted them to be saved. This means he wanted them to be delivered from the consequences of their sin. As we shall see in some of the following readings, breaking the law of God, which is what sin is, puts all men and women under the wrath and judgement of the holy God. This means that unless they are saved, they will spend eternity in hell facing the punishment their sin deserves. It is this truth that makes salvation absolutely essential and desperately urgent.

Ignorance

So what prevented these Israelites from being saved? They were not atheists or agnostics but people who were zealous for God (v. 2). Their problem was ignorance. Their zeal was not based on knowledge. The sort of knowledge to which Paul refers has nothing to do with a person's intellectual ability. It is a knowledge that a child can possess. Neither was their ignorance the result of the truth being hidden from them. They were ignorant in the presence of knowledge. The last verse of Romans 10 is a quotation from the Old Testament, from Isaiah 65:2: 'All day long I have held out my hands to a disobedient and obstinate people.' If you look up that verse in Isaiah you will see that it goes on to say, '... people, who walk in ways not good, pursuing their own imaginations'.

It does not matter where a person begins the journey of faith — whether as an atheist, agnostic, or a deeply religious man or woman. What is common to all men when they think about God is what Paul calls 'zeal ... not based on knowledge', and what Isaiah describes as 'pursuing their own imaginations'. The atheist says, 'There is no God.' The agnostic says, 'It is not possible to know.' The religious person says, 'There is a God and this is how I perceive him to be.' Basically there is little or no difference in any of these three responses. All three are men making pronouncements about God.

Listen to God

The Bible message says to us, 'Stop talking, be quiet and listen to what God has to say: "Faith comes from hearing the message, and the message is heard through the word of Christ"' (v. 17). The Israelites, though deeply religious, were not listening to God. Because of this they did not know the true message of the gospel and had concocted a way of salvation that was unacceptable to God (v. 3).

This compulsive tendency in man to produce a do-it-yourself way of salvation is one of the major obstacles to a true faith in God. Wherever it is present there will inevitably be a rejection of God's way of salvation. It is this rejection that Isaiah laments over when he says, 'Lord, who has believed our message?', which Paul quotes in verse 16. The message Isaiah is referring to is the message of the gospel, the message of a crucified Saviour. This is the message the Scriptures proclaim clearly and incisively, Consequently saving faith will be the result of hearing and believing this message.

God's way of salvation is through the Lord Jesus Christ, so if you want to be saved you must go to the Bible and read there what it has to say about him. And notice also in verses 14 and 15 how Paul stresses the importance of the preaching of the message of salvation. So go to a church where the Bible is believed and preached. There is no salvation apart from the Lord Jesus Christ, and salvation is described in verse 9 as confessing with your mouth that 'Jesus is Lord', and believing in your heart that God raised him from the dead. We shall see what this means in later readings, but note at this point that we are to believe what the Bible says about Christ, and not ideas about, or concepts of, him that originate in our own minds, or someone else's.

The Jesus of Scripture is the incarnate God, born of a virgin, who lived a sinless life, died on the cross to atone for the sin of his people, arose from the dead on the third day, ascended to heaven and will one day return to this world.

God's holiness

The Bible tells us many things about God. It speaks with enthusiasm of his love, wisdom, mercy, goodness etc., but the truth about God that is emphasized above all others is that God is holy. Holiness means not only an absence of all moral evil, but also the presence of an absolute moral perfection. God is holy and that in and of itself makes him totally different from man. But it is also man's greatest problem.

Because God is holy he cannot and will not tolerate sin. This puts man the sinner in a hopeless and impossible position. How can he ever be acceptable to a holy God? The person seeking salvation will soon become aware of this dilemma. It is not just that his sin separates him from God, but God's holiness is also for the sinner an immense problem. The hymn-writer Thomas Binney expressed it like this:

Oh, how shall I, whose native sphere
Is dark, whose mind is dim,

Before the ineffable appear,
And on my naked spirit bear
The uncreated beam?

Left to ourselves it would be hopeless and impossible, but in the matter of salvation God does not leave us to ourselves. He saves, and the fact of his holiness only exalts the merit and worth of the salvation he gives us. That such a God could love and save such miserable sinners as us, is indeed a miracle of grace. So as you read today's chapter bear this in mind.

'Holy, holy, holy…'

Isaiah is allowed to see a vision of the Lord. He sees God on his throne, high and exalted. He sees also the response of the angelic beings to God. They are overwhelmed by the awareness of divine holiness and cannot resist calling to each other, 'Holy, holy, holy is the Lord Almighty.'

You will probably never have such a vision, but you need to appreciate the truth expressed in this chapter. God is not like us. He is not 'one of the boys', and should not be treated with a flippant familiarity. There is an awesome majesty about God that sinners need to respect and fear. This is why Jesus tells us in Luke 12:4, 'Do not be afraid of those who kill the body and after that can do no more. But I will show you whom you should fear: Fear him who, after the killing of the body, has power to throw you into hell. Yes, I tell you, fear him.'

When Isaiah began to realize who and what God is, his response in verse 5 was inevitable. His own sin and unworthiness were exposed in the light of God's holiness. Remember, these words were uttered by a man who was a prophet of God and was probably one of the best and godliest men in the land. Compared to other men Isaiah was as good as any, but he was now seeing himself in relationship to the unutterable purity of God. Sin is wrong and repulsive, not because it fails to meet the standards of society, but because it is an offence against the holiness of God.

The divine yardstick

Have you ever measured yourself by this yardstick? To see ourselves through the lens of divine holiness gives the only accurate assessment of what we are. This is not a recipe for despair. By this standard we will feel ruined and unclean, but such an estimation ought to deliver us once and for all from the do-it-yourself concept of salvation. We are then thrown totally upon the mercy of God, and that is the safest place for a sinner to be.

Verses 6 and 7 encourage us to believe that there is mercy with the Lord. There was for Isaiah, and there is for all who come to God in repentance and faith.

God's love

The fact that God is holy makes it impossible for him to tolerate sin. So in effect it is his holiness that makes salvation so necessary. But God's holiness does not save us; it is God's love that saves from the consequences of sin through the giving of the Lord Jesus Christ to be our Saviour.

In today's reading a religious leader named Nicodemus is totally bewildered by Christ's teaching on God's way of salvation. He cannot understand spiritual concepts and interprets them in a literal way that makes them appear nonsense (v. 4). Jesus explodes a theological bomb in his mind when he tells him, 'You must be born again.' This shatters Nicodemus and he totters in utter confusion and misunderstanding.

Most of us react in a similar way to the gospel when we first hear it, but fortunately for us, God does not leave us there. Man in sin is always in confusion about God and our only hope is that God loves sinners. Verse 16 of today's chapter is a thrilling description of God's love.

God's initiative

God's love, like his holiness, destroys the myth that the sinner can save himself. The gospel starts with an activity of God, 'God so loved the world,' and then demands a response from man: 'whoever believes in him...' The order is important. Man is called upon to respond to an action of God. The initiative is God's. If God had done nothing to save us, then we could do nothing. That is why being born again is so essential. If a person is not born again he or she is spiritually dead and cannot understand spiritual truths or respond to the grace and mercy of God. Being born again is God giving new life to a person who is dead in sin. This is a *must*; without it nothing else is spiritually possible, and it is the love of God that initiates it.

Our response to God would be impossible if God had not first of all shown love to us. John, in his first epistle, spells this out clearly for us: 'This is love; not that we loved God, but that he loved us and sent his Son as an atoning sacrifice for our sins... We love because he first loved us' (1 John 4:10,19).

Love divine

God's love for us is not pity or sentiment, but intensely practical, because it motivates him to deal with our greatest problem. Man in sin is condemned already before the holy God (v. 18). The sinner loves darkness; his deeds are evil; he hates the light (vv. 19-20). This puts him in the position of perishing (v. 16). It is clear from the illustration Jesus uses in verses 14 and 15 (see Numbers 21) that when he speaks of 'perishing' he means the judgement of God's wrath upon sin.

God deals with sin by giving his Son, the Lord Jesus Christ, to die for us. Jesus was made responsible for our sin and took its guilt and punishment. On the cross he faced the judgement and wrath of God instead of his people.

That God should love us so much as to do this is staggering. It is love undeserved, and certainly unmerited, and as John has stressed in the verses quoted above from his epistle, it is love that was unsought by us. John also describes this love of God as being lavished upon us (1 John 3:1). 'Lavished' speaks of abundance, and tells us that God's love is no small thing, but a love unimaginable in its beauty and depth. It is this lavished love that enabled God to give his only Son to die instead of hell-deserving sinners.

Our response

This love demands a response from us. The hymn says:

> Love so amazing, so divine,
> Demands my soul, my life, my all.

Such a response is both sensible and reasonable. The sinner's only hope is in what God has done for him or her. To be condemned already and under the judgement of God is to be in a terrible situation. Therefore to receive, gladly and humbly, a full pardon and eternal life would seem to be most sensible and reasonable. Have you done this? Have you come in repentance and faith to God and received his gift of eternal life?

Jesus — his incarnation

The word used to describe the birth of Jesus is 'incarnation'. It means 'in the flesh', and expresses the amazing truth that when Jesus was born, God became man. In the opening chapter of his Gospel John says, referring to Jesus, 'The Word was God'; then he goes on to declare, 'The Word became flesh and made his dwelling among us.'

The birth of Jesus was very special. The Old Testament prophet Isaiah and the New Testament writers Matthew and Luke all tell us that his mother was a virgin. His birth was not the result of human love, or lust, but came about through the remarkable life-giving operation of the Holy Spirit.

In today's reading we are told why this was necessary and what it all means. In Hebrews 2:14-18 we have one of the clearest statements in the New Testament regarding the reason for God becoming man in the person of the Lord Jesus Christ.

For this reason

In verse 13 we have a quote from Isaiah 8:18, which is part of a Messianic passage, which means it refers to Christ. This is clear from today's reading, where the Old Testament verses quoted in verses 12 and 13 are all attributed to Jesus: 'He says...' So 'the children God has given me' refers to the people that God is going to save through Jesus Christ. Jesus said in John 17:2 that he would give eternal life to all those that God had given him.

These children, those whom God is going to save, are flesh and blood — they are human beings. But God is not flesh and blood; he is not human. So in order to save us he became human. Notice that this truth is repeated again in verses 16 and 17. God does not save angels but human beings: 'For this reason he had to be made like his brothers in every way.'

Why was this necessary? Salvation was planned in heaven but it could not be accomplished in heaven. Atonement for sin must be made to God by man's representative. But there was no man qualified to do this, for all men are sinners. So the eternal God became man, 'so that by his death' (v. 14) he might accomplish salvation for his people. God became man so that as the man Jesus he could die for his people and purchase their salvation. Paul puts it like this in Romans 5:17: 'For if, by the trespass of the one man [Adam], death reigned through that one man, how much more will those who

receive God's abundant provision of grace and of the gift
of righteousness reign in life through the one man, Jesus
Christ.'

Five reasons

In Hebrews 2:14-18 there are five reasons given why God
became man:

1. So that by his death he could conquer the
power of the devil (v. 14)
2. So that he could free his people from the fear
of death (v. 15).
3. So that he could become our High Priest (v.
17).
4. So that he could atone for our sin (v. 17).
5. So that he could help us in our temptations (v.
18).

The accomplishment of all these things meant the
suffering and death of the Son of God. Therefore God had
to become man. John Owen, the Puritan, said, 'The first
and principal end of the Lord Christ's assuming human
nature, was not to reign in it, but to suffer and die in it.'
The incarnation was essential for our salvation because salvation is not a whitewash job. It is not a quick
cover-up. Salvation is the mighty work of God whereby

he makes new men with a new nature. But if we are to be made like him, he must first be made like us (but without sin). If we are to be made partakers of the divine nature, God must first partake of human nature (but not fallen human nature).

Christ Jesus
who being in very nature God,
... made himself nothing,
   taking the very nature of a servant,
   being made in human likeness.
And being found in appearance as a man,
   he humbled himself
   and became obedient to death — even death on
    a cross

                 (Philippians 2:5-8).

Jesus — his deity

The New Testament stresses over and over again the uniqueness and exclusiveness of the Lord Jesus Christ. There is no one like Jesus and it is because of who he is that he alone is able to be our Saviour. If Jesus was merely a human being like the rest of us, he would be a sinner like the rest of us and, like all sinners, would have been under the judgement and wrath of God. If that was true then Jesus could no more save sinners than you or I could. But we concluded yesterday's reading with a quotation from Philippians 2 which tells us that Christ Jesus was in very nature God. This tremendous truth is worked out in more detail in today's reading.

The supremacy of Christ

In verses 13 and 14 Jesus is set before us as the Saviour. God rescues us from sin through his Son, and it is by the

Son that we have redemption and the forgiveness of sins. Paul immediately goes on in verses 15-20 to tell us of the supremacy of Christ. This supremacy is stated powerfully in verse 15. Jesus is the image of the invisible God. There is no one like Jesus because Jesus is God.

An image is nothing unless it is a reflection of an object in one form or another. The gods of the pagans were images, but images of what? Some idea certainly, or some concept, and very often they reflected some fear. Men may even try to make images of the true God, but in so doing they deface the glory of the immortal God (Romans 1:23).

Man was created in the image of God, but that image has been shattered by sin. Now in Jesus we have the perfect reflection of God and this is possible because only one who was equal with God could perfectly interpret and reflect God. The image that Jesus brought us of God was not just a copy, but the real thing. Paul says in verse 19, 'God was pleased to have all his fulness dwell in him.' And he repeats the same truth in verse 9 of chapter 2: 'For in Christ all the fulness of the Deity lives in bodily form.'

The uniqueness of Christ

Throughout history there have been many great men of God and they have in different ways brought us the message of God, and in their own characters have reflected something of the character of God. But none of them was called the image of God, because in all these reflections there was sin and therefore there were flaws and distortion. Jesus alone is the image of God because in him was no sin and the image he puts before us has no flaws or distortions. He is God.

If you were to ask, 'What is God like?' the answer the Bible would give is that he is like Jesus — holy, righteous, just, full of compassion and mercy. He loves sinners and stretches out his arms in love and grace to them, calling upon them to come to him.

On this great truth of who Jesus is rests the sinner's only hope of salvation because God can only be known through the Lord Jesus Christ. When Jesus said, 'I am the way and the truth and the life. No one comes to the Father except through me' (John 14:6), he was not being bigoted but merely stating the truth. And when the apostle Peter, speaking of Jesus, said, 'Salvation is found in no one else, for there is no other name under heaven given to men by which we must be saved' (Acts 4:12), he was not being carried away with an exaggerated enthusiasm, but only declaring to us the truth of the supremacy and uniqueness of the Lord Jesus Christ.

Jesus — the good shepherd

In the allegory of the Good Shepherd Jesus shows clearly why he came into the world and what he alone is able to do for us. He paints a picture of sheep and three different groups of people who are seeking to lead and direct them — thieves, hired hands and the Good Shepherd.

The thief and the hired hand are not really interested in the welfare of the sheep. One is out to steal them and the other deserts them when things get tough (vv. 12-13).

In contrast the Good Shepherd:

owns the sheep (v. 4);
knows each sheep by name and has a personal interest in each of them (v. 3);
loves each sheep so much that he is willing to give his life for them (v.11).

'All we like sheep...'

Why does Jesus tell this allegory and what is its meaning?

Because people are like sheep. Notice, in verse 9 Jesus stops talking about sheep and refers instead to people who need to be saved. In the Old Testament, Isaiah said that all people are like sheep and have gone astray from God. He meant that we are easily led and influenced. This is still as true today as ever it was thousands of years ago. In fact it is even more obvious today.

Vast millions are spent today in advertising to tell people that they will be happier, fitter, lovelier, slimmer, if they buy such and such goods. And it works! Irrespective of how good the product is, good advertising will sell it. That is because by nature the consumer is a sheep and is easily led and influenced. Advertising and packaging work very effectively because of man's sheeplike nature.

But, of course, it is more serious than that. Each person has an immortal soul and that soul is lost. Like sheep we get lost; only in our case we are born already lost, born with a nature in rebellion against God.

Your soul is your most precious possession, but it is lost. It is precious because it is eternal and Jesus said, 'What good will it be for a man if he gains the whole world, yet forfeits his soul?' Do you value your soul? If you don't there are those who do and they are seeking to lead you astray. Jesus said they are like thieves and hired hands. They don't love you, but neither do they ignore you, and they seek to lead your soul to destruction. The reality of this is obvious if you just look at the influences in your life all working to keep you away from God.

The Shepherd Saviour

Praise God there is one who does love you, one who knows all about you and is willing to give his life for you. That Good Shepherd left heaven and came to this world for his sheep. He came to seek and save the lost.

To 'save' means to deliver us from the consequences of our sin. He desires to give us a new nature that wants and loves God. The only way the Good Shepherd could do this was by dying for his sheep (v. 11). This means that on the cross Jesus paid the debt you had incurred by breaking the law of God. The wages of sin is death and Jesus died for his sheep. This death of Jesus the Good Shepherd is described in a most glorious way in verse 18.

It was an act of voluntary love. Jesus was not forced onto the cross against his will by his enemies. There was no power in existence that could have done this. The death of Jesus was a sacrifice, a giving of himself to die instead of his people, and in this act Jesus the Son was in perfect accord with the wishes of God the Father. But the sacrifice for sin was not to be the end. Jesus not only had authority or power to lay down his life but power to take it up again. This he did on the third day when he arose from the grave victor over sin and death.

The Holy Spirit in salvation

God's plan of salvation in sending the Lord Jesus Christ into the world to be our Saviour was no hit-or-miss venture. God's plan was not to make salvation possible and then hope that some sinners somewhere might benefit from it. Jesus came into the world to definitely seek and save the lost, and to gather to himself a people. For salvation to be accomplished it was necessary for Jesus to die for us and to rise again from the dead, and it is also necessary for the Holy Spirit to make the gospel real to us as individuals. This is why Jesus said in verse 7 of today's passage that it was good for him to leave us, to go back to heaven. Once Christ had ascended to heaven God would send the Holy Spirit to us.

Without the work of the Holy Spirit salvation would be impossible. The Holy Spirit is not just an influence, but the Third Person of the Trinity, and therefore like Jesus he is divine. God the Holy Spirit is as essential to our salvation as are God the Father and God the Son.

In planning salvation God did not underestimate the grip of sin on the hearts of men and women. He knew it was not enough just to make salvation possible. If sinners are to be saved then God must save them. He must do all that is needed. So after God the Father planned salvation and God the Son purchased it for us, God the Holy Spirit works in the hearts of sinners to convict of sin and bring us in repentance and faith to God. In today's reading Jesus tells us of the Spirit's work of conviction. He comes to convict the world of guilt in regard to three things: sin, righteousness and judgement. The sin we all need to be convicted of is our own, the righteousness is Christ's and the judgement is God's.

Sin

If people think of sin at all they usually think of it in terms of some shameful act against society, but when the Holy Spirit convicts of sin he reveals to men and women something which they consider to be unimportant. This sin is that of not believing in the Lord Jesus Christ (v. 9). The Holy Spirit does this by fixing in a person's mind the meaning and evidence of the truth about Jesus. Then he produces in the mind and heart the conviction that by not believing these truths there is great sin. Unbelief is not merely a wrong opinion, or an intellectual mistake, but deep, aggravated sin — the greatest sin a man or woman is capable of committing.

33

A person may be convicted that he is a liar, a thief, a cheat, or even a murderer, but unless he is convicted of this sin of unbelief he will never know salvation and peace with God.

Righteousness

The Holy Spirit convicts sinners of Christ's righteousness — that is, of his unique and incomparable qualifications to deal with our sin. He does this in several ways, by revealing to us the character of Jesus and the truth of his teaching and miracles. But in verse 10 Jesus mentions one way above all others: 'because I am going to the Father'.

The world rejected Jesus as a fraud but his resurrection and ascension provided the infallible truth that all he said and claimed was right. He said he would rise from the dead and ascend to heaven, and he did. These claims were not things that it was possible to manufacture or falsify.

In order to be saved a sinner needs to believe in the uniqueness of Jesus. He is the only Saviour.

Judgement

The judgement mentioned in verse 11 is God's judgement of the prince of this world, that is, of the devil. The reference is to the cross. The Spirit convicts men that the cross was a victory for God and that the devil was defeated there. Jesus, by his life, death and resurrection, has defeated, judged and cast out the devil.

There is a pattern in all this. A man is not concerned at all about the righteousness of Christ and the judgement of God until he is first convicted of his own sin. Once convicted he longs for a Saviour and it is then time to point him to Jesus, the Righteous One who alone is able to deal with sin.

Man's sin and need

The fact of sin

If you do not understand Genesis 3 you will never understand the gospel. Everything else that follows in the Bible does so as a consequence of the events that took place in the Garden of Eden. And they were events, not myths. Underlying all the actions of Jesus and all the teaching of the New Testament is the fact of human sin and the doctrine of the fall of man. By the Fall we mean man's fall from the perfect condition in which he was created into a state of sin.

Relevance for today

The relevance of this chapter for today's men and women is easy to see. Deep in all our hearts is a yearning for the forbidden fruit, and coupled with this is a distrust of God's Word. It is much easier to believe Satan's whispered insinuations than God's clear declarations.

Adam and Eve were made by God and for God. They were meant to enjoy God, and they did. Everything necessary for life and happiness was given to them. Only one thing was forbidden (vv. 2-3) and that was something they did not need; nor did they want it until they began to listen to Satan. They fell for the lies of the Evil One and this led to sin becoming part of their human nature for the first time.

In the Fall man lost essentially three things:

1. Peace with God. He is now afraid of God and hides from him (v. 10).

2. Access to God. He is now banned from the presence of God and a cherubim was placed at the gate of the Garden of Eden with a flaming sword in his hand to prevent Adam and Eve from coming into the holy presence of God (v. 24).

3. Hope for the future. From now on the whole of man's lifestyle is changed and the future holds nothing but sweat and tears (vv.17-19).

Sin has left its devastating imprint upon human nature from Adam down to us, and what was true of Adam is still true of us (see Romans 5:12-21): the sinner has no peace with God, no access to God and no hope for the future.

Human responsibility

It is clear from Genesis 3 that behind sin is the activity of
Satan, but this does not excuse us, or remove our responsibility for our actions. The sin of Eve in verse 6 was a
result of her listening to the lies of Satan. It is obvious
from verse 2 that she knew exactly what God had said but
she chose to ignore this. And when Satan questioned the
integrity and character of God in verse 5, she knew from
an abundant experience of God's goodness to her and
Adam that this was an enormous lie, but she still listened.
Satan lied, but Eve sinned. It was she, not Satan, who took
and ate the forbidden fruit, and Adam followed his wife's
example. They were responsible for their own sin and
God's judgement fell on them as well as on the serpent.
This responsibility we, like Adam and Eve, have always
been reluctant to accept. Adam blamed Eve (v. 12) and
Eve blamed the serpent (v. 13), and ever since we have
been blaming everyone and everything for our sin. 'It's
not our fault,' we say. 'It's our environment, our upbringing, our parents.' But God holds us responsible and there
is no escaping that.

A promised Saviour

Sin has left man in a helpless and hopeless position. Our
only hope is the grace and love of God, and this emerges

in this sad chapter in verse 15. Here is the first Bible promise of a Saviour and it began to be fulfilled when God became man in the person of the Lord Jesus Christ. Our only hope as sinners is to be found in Christ. All we lost in the Fall — peace with God, access to God and a future hope — is restored to us in Christ when we know him as our Saviour: 'Therefore, since we have been justified through faith, we have peace with God through our Lord Jesus Christ, through whom we have gained access by faith into this grace in which we now stand. And we rejoice in the hope of the glory of God' (Rom. 5:1-2).

The effects of sin

Yesterday we saw the catastrophic effect sin had when it entered the natures of Adam and Eve. Nothing was ever the same again. That was bad enough, but in Genesis 4 we are shown that sin's power was not confined to Adam and Eve: it also polluted the nature of their children. And it does not finish there: 'Therefore, just as sin entered the world through one man, and death through sin, and in this way death comes to all men, because all sin' (Romans 5:12).

Sin pollutes all people

Perhaps Adam and Eve thought that with the birth of a son things would be different. They remembered the promise of God that salvation from the power of sin would come through the woman's offspring. Well, here was the offspring and Eve declared, perhaps with hope and excitement, that the birth was with the help of the Lord. As they held the newborn baby they probably thought that he would be the deliverer. Instead he became a murderer and the sad history of humanity written in blood had begun. By the time we reach Genesis 6 all the descendants of Adam, the whole of mankind, are showing the effects of sin: 'The Lord saw how great man's wickedness on the earth had become, and that every inclination of the thoughts of his heart was only evil all the time' (Genesis 6:5).

Sadly the Cain and Abel story was no one-off event, but part of the continual and ongoing testimony to the effects of sin in the human heart. Sin is not merely a social disease. It is not just an explanation of how badly we behave to each other, but primarily it is a demonstration of man's hostility to God. If man cannot get his relationship with God right, he will never be right with his fellow man. That is why Jesus said that the greatest commandment is to 'Love the Lord your God with all your heart and with all your soul and with all your mind.' The Saviour went on to say that the second greatest commandment is: 'Love your neighbour as yourself' (Matthew 22:37-39). We must get the first right before we have any hope of succeeding with the second.

Sinners approaching God

It was exactly at this point that Cain failed. His relationship with God was all wrong, as is revealed in verses 3-

44

7. Here we see two men approaching God in worship. On the surface they seem similar. They are brothers, with the same parents, the same upbringing and the same advantages. There are obviously some differences in that Cain worked the soil and Abel looked after the animals. But there is a greater difference which is only revealed when they seek to come to God, and the true worth of a man is only to be measured in terms of what God thinks of him.

When any man approaches God he must do so as a sinner, as one who has no rights. He comes aware of his sin and guilt, and this will govern how he approaches God. We are told in Hebrews 11:4, 'By faith Abel offered God a better sacrifice than Cain did.' It was the difference in the sacrifice, or offering, that these brothers brought to God that caused one to be accepted and the other rejected. The offerings were indicative of their attitude to God. Abel came conscious of his sin and the need for that sin to be atoned for. He came in God's way, trusting in the sacrifice of shed blood. Cain was different. He wilfully ignored the consequences of the Fall. His offering of fruit merely acknowledged God as Creator and sustainer of life, whereas saving faith is pre-eminently faith in the redemptive love of God.

Cain was very angry at his rejection by God and that anger spilled over against his brother. God warned him of the effects both of his worthless offering and his burning anger: 'Sin is crouching at your door; it desires to have you, but you must master it' (vv. 6-7). Sadly, Cain did not master it and the end result was the murder of his brother.

45

The gospel

In Genesis 3 and 4 we have a simple but clear illustration of the gospel. The whole human race sinned in Adam and the wages of that sin is death. Either I, the sinner, must accept those wages and suffer death and hell, or someone else, an innocent substitute on whom death has no claim, must be paid those wages instead of me. Jesus is the substitute. God laid on him our sin and guilt, so when we come to God we must come, like Abel, with the right offering. The Lord looked with favour on Abel and his offering, and the Lord looks with favour on us when we come trusting in the atoning death of Jesus, the Lamb of God.

The consequences of sin

In today's reading Paul is writing of people who had not received the full revelation of God through the Lord Jesus Christ. The apostle does not refer to God as Saviour but as Creator and Lawgiver, and he does not mention Christ at all. These were people who had never heard the gospel, but none the less they were under the judgement and wrath of God. They were without excuse for their sin (v. 20) because God's revelation of himself in nature was enough to cause people to know the truth about him (vv. 19-20).

If the wrath of God came upon these people, how much more will it come upon those of us who have received the full glory of gospel truths in Christ? If they were without excuse, how much more so are we? These people lived in complete disregard for the law of God. They knew the truth but suppressed it (v. 18), twisted it and eventually ignored it. All this inevitably leads up to the terrible situation described in verses 21-23.

To these people came the wrath of God, but it did not come as in the days of Noah with a flood, or as in the days of Sodom and Gomorrah with fire and brimstone. God's wrath came here in the far more terrible way described in verses 24, 26 and 28: 'God gave them over...' God withdrew his restraining hand upon sin and let these people wallow in it.

Sin's reality today

Though they were written about people living hundreds of years ago, these words could well be describing to-day's society.

1. There is an almost total rejection of God (v. 21).

2. Men are wise enough to put men on the moon, but foolish enough for all the violence, wars and crime of our age (v. 22).

3. Today we see abuse of God openly flouted as God and Jesus are made the subject of laughter and scorned (v. 23)

4. Men and women degrade their bodies with sex, drink and drugs (v. 24).

5. Rampant homosexuality and lesbianism are as blatant today as they were in Sodom (vv. 26-27).

6. In nations that were built upon the Christian ethic, the knowledge and law of God are no longer retained and all sorts of laws are passed to legalize what God forbids (v. 28).

All this is very real today in nations that were once called Christian. It is no wonder that we too are experiencing the wrath of God.

A just punishment

God's wrath is his anger against sin and his determination to punish it. It is divine holiness stirred into action against violations of his holy law. God, who is utterly and completely holy, cannot regard evil and good as the same. He cannot smile benevolently upon both truth and lies. So God's holiness makes hell as inevitable as his love makes heaven.

God never excuses sin. The cross proves that. On the cross sin is punished as it is borne by our substitute, the Lord Jesus Christ. No sin is excusable but, thank God, it is pardonable in Christ. However, the point that today's reading is making is that God always deals with sin. He deals with it now — 'The wrath of God is being revealed' (v. 18) is in the present tense — and he will deal with it once and for all on what the Bible calls the Day of Judgement.

49

God's wrath is as real as his love, but it is not like human wrath. It is not vindictive, capricious or irrational. It is a right and necessary reaction against moral evil. It is judicial wrath against guilty sinners and God is only angry when anger is called for.

No one is good

In verse 10 of today's reading Paul states that there is no one righteous and then, so that there can be no possibility of misunderstanding what he means, he adds the words: 'not even one'. He does the same thing in verse 12: 'There is no one who does good, not even one.'

It is clear enough what the apostle is saying, but perhaps we are inclined to think that this is an absurd generalization. Paul must be overstating the case because we know many good people. What about those folk like Mother Theresa who give their lives to help the poor? It does seem as if Paul is wrong here. But all he is doing is quoting from Psalm 14. So are both Paul and David the psalmist wrong? If they are, then so too is Jesus, because he said exactly the same thing in Mark 10:18: 'No one is good, except God alone.'

What does 'good' mean?

Obviously there is a difference between the way we use
the word 'good' and the way Jesus, Paul and David used
it. That is exactly what Jesus is saying to the young man
who came to him asking, 'What must I do to inherit
eternal life?' This man's concept of goodness was typical
of many today. He had cast a careless glance over his life
and was quite satisfied with his external respectability.
When Jesus said to him that no one was good except God,
the Saviour was cutting at the root of the common notion
of self-achieved goodness.

Our definition of goodness is merely to compare one
person with another, or with what society considers right
and proper. God's definition is to compare us with his
holy, sinless self. By that standard Psalm 14 and Romans
3 are perfectly true. All goodness stems only from a living
relationship with God. Hence when in Acts 11:24
Barnabas is called a good man, it is because he was filled
with the Holy Spirit and faith.

Where does this leave us? Are we still making the
mistake of the young man in Mark 10, or are we beginning
to see the truth expressed by Jesus, Paul and David that
there is no one good?

Unacceptable to God

What does this mean in practical terms? It means that there is no one acceptable to God on terms of his or her own merit. It means that left to ourselves we would never understand God or seek God (v. 11). We would not be at peace with God (v. 17) and would have no fear of God (v. 18). It means that you are unacceptable to God. No matter what you do, God will never regard you as good or righteous (v. 20). That is the terrible condition that sin has put us all in. Most sinners react strongly against this biblical truth when they are first confronted with it. It offends our pride and self-esteem, but we need to take it seriously.

Imagine that you bought a new radio. You take it home and switch it on, but the reception is very poor. It is so full of interference that you cannot hear the programmes clearly. So you take it back to the shop and say, 'This is no good. It will not do what it was made to do and claims to do. It is no good and therefore unacceptable to me.' God looks at us in the same way. When he created man he said, 'This is very good.' Then sin came and God now says of man, 'There is no one good.' Man will not do what he was made to do, that is to know and enjoy God. 'No good' means that we are unacceptable to God. But God cannot take us back to the shop and change us, as we would do with a faulty radio. So what does God do? He makes us acceptable by giving us a goodness, a righteousness, that is not our own. That is what Paul says in verses 21 and 22, and we shall see more of this in later readings.

For the moment, consider seriously what God is saying to you in today's reading. Believe it and stop protesting that you are not as bad as many other people. You are a sinner; forget others for a moment. That sin puts *you* under the wrath of God. The Scripture says this to you to silence your protests (v. 19). You are guilty before God. The case is overwhelmingly proved, so stop protesting your innocence and cry to God for the mercy that Paul brings before us in the rest of Romans 3.

Goodness is not enough

In spite of what we saw in yesterday's reading many people still insist that they can earn their salvation by religious observance or moral and social activities. Salvation by works is a very popular doctrine. Acts chapters 10 and 11 tell us the story of Cornelius, and if ever a man was good it was this man. If ever a man could have been saved by his own actions, this was the man, but as verse 14 of our reading shows us, he had to be saved by hearing the message of the gospel.

A sincere man

Cornelius was a Roman centurion of some standing (10:1) but, more importantly, we are told that he was 'devout and God-fearing; he gave generously to those in need and prayed to God regularly' (10:2). He believed in the one God, the Creator of heaven and earth, and he sought to worship this God and to live his life in a right and proper fear of God. His religion was devout, not casual or nominal.

So here was a man sincere, devout and earnest, but still he was an unenlightened soul groping for God. It is clear from 10:4 that God is impressed with this man. He is impressed with a man living according to the light and understanding he has. But God does not leave him there. Cornelius needs to hear the gospel; this is why the Lord in his love and mercy arranges for this Roman to meet Peter. From Peter he will hear the 'message through which you and all your household will be saved' (11:14). This is a very important verse. It is not Cornelius' good life and genuine religious convictions that are going to save him, but the gospel of the Lord Jesus Christ. In other words, though God is impressed with Cornelius, he still treats him as a sinner because in spite of all his good works he is still a sinner who needs saving.

Here is a remarkable man. If any man could be acceptable to God apart from faith in Christ, this is the one. A better specimen of humanity would be hard to find, but God treats him as a sinner who needs to hear and believe the gospel.

What does it mean to be saved?

It means to be delivered from the guilt and punishment our sins have incurred. The Bible says that all have sinned, therefore all need to be saved. But how can a sinner be saved?

Ephesians 2 tells us that salvation is by grace through faith in Christ.

Romans 10 tells us that faith comes from hearing the Word of God. In the ordinary process of events it would not have been very likely that Cornelius would have heard the gospel. So God sets in motion an extraordinary series of events to ensure that this man hears the truth. First there was a vision of an angel to Cornelius (10:3-6), then Peter's amazing vision of the sheet let down from heaven (10:9-16). Both these events were designed to make Peter willing to preach to Cornelius and Cornelius anxious to hear Peter's preaching.

Why did God do all this? Because sinners need to hear the gospel. It is words, not works, that save, but they have to be the words of eternal life that are found only in the message of Jesus.

Do you want to be saved? Then believe this now: you can do nothing to save yourself.

This truth is clearly demonstrated in the life of Cornelius. So if you cannot save yourself you are left, as was this Roman centurion, only with the gospel. But you could be left in no better place providing you hear the Word of God as Cornelius did: 'Now we are all here in the presence of God to listen to everything the Lord has commanded you to tell us' (10:33)

There are three essential things in this story that led up to the salvation of Cornelius:

1. The goodness of God in bringing the gospel to him.

2. The faithful preaching of Peter.

3. An eagerness to hear and submit to the authority of the Word of God.

God's way of salvation

Old Testament pictures — The Day of Atonement

God's way of salvation did not start in the New Testament when Jesus came into the world. From time to time in the Old Testament the Lord designed certain events to be pictures of what Jesus was going to do when he came. For instance, today's reading describing the Day of Atonement is clearly expounded in Hebrews chapters 9 and 10 in terms of the death of our Saviour.

Approaching God

Verse 1 of today's reading reveals what a serious business it is for sinners to approach the holy God. Aaron's sons, Nadab and Abihu, were priests but that did not mean they could approach God in worship in any way they liked. We are told in Leviticus 10:1 that 'They offered unauthorized fire before the Lord contrary to his command.' What exactly this involved we do not know but it was contrary to God's prescribed way and they died because of it. So God warns Aaron in Leviticus 16:2 that he is not to come into the Most Holy Place whenever he chooses or he too will die.

The Most Holy Place, or Holy of Holies, was the small room in the Tent of Meeting, or tabernacle, where the Ark of the Covenant was kept. The lid of the ark was called the mercy seat, and in this small room God's presence was deemed to be known in a special way. Therefore it was not to be entered lightly and only the high priest was allowed in, and then only once a year on the Day of Atonement. If the mercy seat was approached in God's prescribed way then there was great blessing for the people, but if it was approached in any other way, it meant death.

All this may sound very strange to us today but it was symbolizing two very important truths that are just as relevant now as they were in the days when Leviticus was written — namely, the unutterable holiness of God and the exceeding sinfulness of man. God wants us to come to him, but our sin is an enormous problem that must be dealt with first. The Old Testament system of sacrifices was instigated by God to remind man that his sin was a barrier. The sacrifice of bulls and goats and lambs was a symbolic way of cleansing the sinner that had one essential common factor: 'Without the shedding of blood there is no forgiveness' (Hebrews 9:22). They could not really deal with sin but served to remind the people of the fact of sin (Hebrews 10:3-4).

Two goats

Several things took place on the Day of Atonement but let us concentrate on the two goats mentioned in verses 7-10 of today's reading. One was killed and its blood was taken by the high priest into the Most Holy Place and sprinkled on the mercy seat. This symbolized the turning away of the wrath of God from man's guilt. Mercy, instead of judgement, came to the sinner.

The other goat, called the scapegoat, was brought to the high priest, who laid his hands on the animal's head and confessed the sin of the people. Symbolically the sins were transferred to the scapegoat and the goat, when sent into the desert, took away the sin of the people (vv. 20-22).

All this was symbolic. They were, says Hebrews 9:10, 'external regulations applying until the time of the new order'. That new order came with the Lord Jesus Christ. What was symbolic on the Day of Atonement became reality in Christ. The death of our Saviour is the only sacrifice that God now recognizes. When Jesus died on the cross he did what both goats symbolized: he turned away the wrath of God from us and he took away our sin. Christ's sacrifice was once for all (Hebrews 10:10).

When men approach God today the only way that is acceptable to the holy God is through the Lord Jesus Christ. We must know that he has dealt once and for all with our sin; only then can we come with confidence into the presence of God.

Old Testament pictures — the Passover

God was determined to set his people free from the slavery of Egypt. Repeatedly he had sent to Egypt's ruler the message to 'Let my people go' (Exodus 10:3). Pharaoh refused to obey even after God had sent nine terrible plagues to Egypt. The Lord had been patient with this hard-hearted Egyptian but 'Now the Lord said to Moses, "I will bring one more plague on Pharaoh and on Egypt. After that, he will let you go from here"' (Exodus 11:1). The tenth plague was that on a given night the angel of death would be sent by the Lord to kill the first-born son in every home in Egypt.

When this terrible event took place God would protect his own people. The Lord would make 'a distinction between Egypt and Israel' (Exodus 11:7), but this would not happen automatically. To benefit from this provision of the grace of God the Israelites had to do as God commanded them in Exodus 12:3-11.

The blood

The blood of the sacrificial lamb sprinkled on the door-frames of the Israelite homes was crucial for their deliverance. God said, 'The blood will be a sign for you on the houses where you are; and when I see the blood, I will pass over you. No destructive plague will touch you when I strike Egypt' (Exodus 12:13).

The first-born in the Israelite homes were spared from the judgement of God that night, not simply because they were Israelites, but because they were sheltering under the blood of the Passover lamb. The distinction that God put between these two peoples was not a national, or cultural, or even religious one. The distinction was of obedience to the revealed purpose and grace of God. The difference between the Egyptians and the Israelites that brought salvation was the blood on the door-frames, for God had promised, 'When I see the blood, I will pass over you.'

Christ our Passover Lamb

The significance of the Old Testament Passover for us today is revealed in many New Testament references — none more so than 1 Corinthians 5:7 where Paul states that 'Christ, our Passover Lamb, has been sacrificed.'

The apostle is saying that the Old Testament event was meant by God to be a picture for us of the meaning of the death of Christ. Jesus is the Lamb of God who shed his blood to deliver us from sin. The apostle Peter tells us clearly that we are redeemed 'with the precious blood of Christ, a lamb without blemish or defect' (1 Peter 1:18-19).

The original Passover delivered the Israelites from the judgement of God and set them free to enjoy new life. They were no longer slaves but free men and women enjoying the provisions and mercy of the Lord. So for us today the death of Christ our Passover delivers us from the guilt and penalty of our sin. In Christ we have new life and can enjoy now all that God has promised his people.

If you are to become a Christian it must be by the way that God has laid down. The Lord God does not say, 'When I see your kindness and generosity and religious observances then I will pass over you in judgement and pardon all your sin.' God's way of salvation is through the blood of Christ, through his atoning death on the cross.

For us today the equivalent of sheltering under the blood is to trust alone in the death of the Lord Jesus Christ to make us acceptable to God. When we do that God's judgement passes over us and our sin and guilt are fully pardoned.

An Old Testament prophecy — Forsaken by God

This psalm was written by David about a thousand years before Christ was born, yet it is more than merely a description of David's experience. This is prophecy and it also describes what is going to happen to the Messiah. 'Messiah' is a Hebrew word and the Greek equivalent is the word 'Christ'. Jesus Christ is the Messiah, and he is going to suffer all that is described in Psalm 22. Compare verse 1 of the psalm with Matthew 27:46; then compare verses 7 and 8 with Matthew 27:41-44 and also verse 18 with Matthew 27:35.

Forsaken by God (vv. 1-5)

Jesus did not merely quote these words on the cross; he experienced them. The testimony of God's people down the centuries is to the absolute faithfulness of God. David said in Psalm 37 that he had never seen the righteous forsaken. There was no one more righteous than Jesus but he was forsaken by God. Psalm 22:4 is the normal experience of God's people — they trust in the Lord and he helps them. So why was Christ forsaken by God the Father?

The explanation is to be found in verse 3: God is the Holy One. We have already in our readings seen something of the holiness of God and if we ever forget this we shall be in danger of failing to understand the true character of God and why he acts as he does.

The holy God laid our sin and guilt upon his Son and Jesus our substitute bore it alone. On the cross he was facing the wrath and judgement of God upon our sin. That is why the Father turned his back on him. The Bible says that God is so holy that he is of purer eyes than to behold evil and cannot look on iniquity. So when Christ bore our sin he was left to tread the winepress of divine wrath alone. There was no angel to help him, no friend to comfort him, no Holy Spirit to assure him, no smile of a heavenly Father to encourage him. Christ hung on the cross alone with our sins, facing all the hatred of the world and hell, but far worse, facing the holy judgement of the Lord upon the sin of his people.

The loneliness and agony of the cross (vv. 6-21)

Jesus is the Lord of glory, the express image of God, yet

in verse 6 he describes himself as a worm and not even a man. It is sin, our sin, that has done this.

In verses 7 and 8 we see this sin erupt into hatred and scorn of Jesus. Verses 14-17 show us the physical agony of the cross. This is the cost of salvation. This is what sin does. At the cross we see man's hatred of God, but we also see God's hatred of sin as the Holy One deals with the sinner's substitute. Sin is an insult to the holiness of God; it separates man from God and leaves him with no hope in the world.

Deliverance (vv. 22-31)

Calvary is past and now we see something of Christ's triumph. The lament of verse 1 turns into the joyful assurance of verse 24: 'He has not hidden his face from him but has listened to his cry for help.' The forsaking was very real but it was only temporary and now sweet communion is once again enjoyed with the heavenly Father. Sin has been dealt with, divine justice is satisfied and now divine love breaks out in the praise of verse 22 and the worship of verse 29.

And note especially the last glorious proclamation of verses 30 and 31. Future generations will be told — told what? Told what Jesus has done on the cross; told of God's love and grace and mercy and provision of salvation; told of Jesus dying in our place.

You have been told the same thing all the way through this book. What do you intend to do about it? Follow the advice of verse 26 and seek the Lord. Seek him for forgiveness and pardon for all your sin. Seek him for love and grace to save you.

The curse of the law

We have seen already that man's greatest problem is his sin and guilt before the holy God. Sin is a problem because it puts us under the curse of the law. The curse of the law is its rightful punishment upon all those who break the law of God. We have all broken that law; therefore we are all under this curse, and without deliverance from it there can be no salvation. We cannot at the same time be under the curse of the law and also be acceptable to God. So what is the answer?

In today's reading Paul gives us the answer in one word — Christ. Christ is the answer because Christ is God's answer. Man's answer is always law — that is, his own efforts. But this does not work. It is our inability to keep God's holy law that is our problem. In verse 10 Paul quotes from Deuteronomy 27:26 and spells out the problem. We are under this curse if we do not continue — that is, *all the time* — to do *everything* — that is, there is to be no failure at all. The law allows for no failure: it must be total obedience every moment of our lives, otherwise we are deemed to be guilty. By that standard we have no hope.

Our only hope is the grace and mercy of God. Because God loved us he sent the Lord Jesus Christ into the world to redeem us from the curse of the law.

Christ became a curse

The statement in verse 13 that Christ became a curse for us is one of the most amazing in the Bible, and immediately we are in the realm of a doctrine that the Bible teaches over and over again — namely, the substitutionary death of Christ for his people. The fact that Paul speaks of Christ becoming a curse reminds us that, unlike us, he was not under the curse of the law. We have seen that Jesus was sinless, so it was not possible in a normal situation for him to be under this curse. But when God laid on him our sin and guilt the consequence of that was that the Son of God became a curse. It was 'for us'. He became responsible for our sin and therefore our curse was also put on Jesus.

The tree

Paul explains this by quoting again from Deuteronomy: 'Cursed is everyone who is hung on a tree' (Deuteronomy

21:23). This Old Testament verse is not referring directly to crucifixion because that means of execution was not known when Moses wrote Deuteronomy. It refers to the taking of the dead body of an executed criminal and nailing it to a tree. This was deemed to be a most terrible thing, a symbol of divine rejection.

A tree is not a cross, but nevertheless on five occasions the New Testament writers speak of the cross as a tree (Galatians 3:13; 1 Peter 2:24; Acts 5:30; 10:39; 13:29). They do this to link the death of Jesus with Deuteronomy 21:23. They are emphasizing the truth that on the cross Christ became a curse for us. He paid the penalty of our violation of God's law. By his death he redeems us from the curse.

Faith

Verse 14 tells us why he redeemed us. The greatest blessing given to Abraham was to hear God saying, 'I will be your God and you will belong to me.' It was the blessing of belonging to God and this becomes ours in salvation.

The way to obtain this blessing, says verse 14, is by faith: not our own efforts, not our goodness, not our morality or religion, but faith in what Christ did for us on the cross. Faith is not a way of achieving salvation; it is the God-appointed way of receiving the gift of salvation. Faith is not a step in the dark: it is the exact opposite; it is a step out of the dark into the light of Christ. Faith looks to Jesus alone. It has stopped trying to save itself and casts itself upon the grace and love of God in Christ for full and free salvation.

Do you have this faith? Because of who Jesus is and what he has done for us, it is a most reasonable act. Stop trying to save yourself and turn to Christ, who is God's answer to your problem of sin.

A righteousness from God

The prime function of the gospel is not to make men happy but to make them righteous. We have seen that there is no one righteous, no one who meets with God's approval and is acceptable to him. A man can be happy and content with his life and have no thought of God and go to hell. But you cannot go to hell if you are righteous because then you are acceptable to God. Being acceptable to God is the greatest happiness anyone can experience.

In verse 21 'a righteousness from God' is not describing something that is a characteristic of God himself, like the love of God or the holiness of God. It means a righteousness that comes from God to us. It is something which God gives us. This is why the gospel is such good news. It does not tell us what we must achieve, but what has been achieved for us, and what we can now receive as a gift from God. When something has to be achieved it will always be out of the reach of some, but a free gift offered to all is a very different thing.

Revealed

In Romans 1:17 the apostle says that this righteousness is revealed in the gospel. The gospel is not man's idea of what religion ought to be. It is not the result of centuries of man's search for God. It is an announcement, or revelation, from God to sinful man that here is the answer to our problem of sin. Here is the only thing that can make guilty sinners acceptable to God.

Notice, in verse 21, that this gift of God is 'apart from law'; that is, it has nothing to do with our achievements. Salvation is not the result of keeping a set of rules but is received by faith.

Justified

Justification by faith is the heart of the Christian gospel. Justification is the sovereign work of God whereby he declares the guilty sinner to be righteous and the rightful demands of the law satisfied.

Let me break down this definition for you:

Sovereign work of God — God does it all; the sinner contributes nothing but his sin.

Declares — the judge pronounces a legal verdict.

Guilty sinner — guilty by nature and guilty by action.

Righteous — right with God.

Demands of the law — God's law demands eternal death for the sinner.

Satisfied — legally and justly satisfied by the atoning death of Christ.

All these truths are spelt out in today's reading. You know you are a sinner or you would never have got this far in reading this book. You may feel that conviction of sin is tearing you to pieces and long to know that it is all forgiven. Then listen to what God is saying in the gospel. Christ has done all that is necessary to deal with your sin. Believe that and come to Christ in repentance and faith for salvation.

What you need is the righteousness that Romans 3 is referring to. Isaiah 61:10 talks of God covering us with garments of salvation and a robe of righteousness. None of us can earn this or do it for ourselves; it is a gift of God's grace and God himself does it. But, we are told in Romans 1:17; 3:22 and Philippians 3:9, this gift comes to us when by faith we cast ourselves upon the mercy of God. Let us be clear on this, we are not saved by our faith. My faith does not make me acceptable to God. Only the righteousness of Christ can do that. Faith is the channel by which Christ's righteousness comes to the sinner.

Reconciled to God

On four occasions in the New Testament Paul writes of
the work and ministry of Christ in terms of reconciliation
(Romans 5:10; Ephesians 2:16; Colossians 1:21 and
today's reading). To reconcile means to remove an en-
mity or quarrel between two people at variance with each
other and to bring them together in peace. In the New
Testament the two parties are God and man: God who is
holy, sinless and pure; and man who is unholy, sinful and
guilty. God and man need reconciling because between
them is the great barrier of sin.

According to Romans 5:10 God and man are enemies.
There is, says Ephesians 2:16, hostility between them and
according to Colossians 1:21 they are alienated. There is
therefore need for reconciliation. Someone must remove
the human sin which is the cause of the hostility. Paul
argues in verse 18 of today's reading that it is God who
does the reconciling and he does it through the Lord Jesus
Christ. In 2 Corinthians 5 reconciliation is described in
four simple but essential steps.

1. God does not count men's sin against them

As we have seen several times in this book, we have all
sinned against God and broken his law. Therefore divine
law quite reasonably and justly demands that its verdict
against sin be carried out.

God begins his work of reconciliation by not counting
our sin against us. We are responsible for our sin and we
should bear its consequences. Each sin is like one of the
individual items on a bill and every time we sin the debt
grows. But in reconciliation God wipes the slate clean; he
removes every debt on the bill, thus leaving us with
nothing to pay.

But what happens to our sins? Are they just forgotten?
No, God cannot do that. These sins have to be answered
for. The debt has to be paid in full and God's holy law
satisfied. So, then, if God does not count our sins against
us, what does he do with them?

2. He counts our sin against Christ

The amazing declaration of the gospel is that God counts
our sin against his Son. He makes Jesus responsible for
our sin (v. 21). Jesus willingly accepts that terrible
responsibility and God lays on him the sin and guilt of his
people.

79

3. Christ bears the punishment that was due to us

Jesus, now bearing our sin, is treated by God as we deserve to be treated and the full wrath of God falls upon our sinbearer on the cross. Sin, which is the barrier, is dealt with legally and decisively.

4. God credits the righteousness of Jesus to us

The last stage in reconciliation is that, having dealt with our sin in Christ, God now counts to us the righteousness of his Son. We become new creations (v. 17) and God is able to treat us as he would normally treat the Lord Jesus. Because our sin is credited to Jesus and Jesus' righteousness is credited to us, the barrier between God and man is dealt with. So Paul urges us, 'Be reconciled to God' (v. 20).

Reconciliation is now possible. God has made it so. Christ has done all that is necessary and God will accept you when you come to him trusting in nothing but what the Lord Jesus Christ has done for you.

By grace

The recurring message of the Bible is that salvation is by grace alone. This is equally true of the Old Testament as of the New. Grace means the undeserved favour of God to sinners who because of their actions deserve the opposite. God was continually showing grace to Israel and without this they would have fared no better than any other nation.

Dead in sin (vv. 1-3)

If the first three verses of today's reading are true then salvation has to be by grace. Here we see the natural condition of all men and women — dead in transgressions and sin. 'Dead' is a very strong word. There are no degrees of deadness. You cannot be half dead. If you are dead you are totally unable to do anything to change your condition. When Paul says we are dead in sin he means we are unable to change our spiritual condition. We are spiritually helpless and hopeless, and if we are to be saved God must do it because we cannot.

But God (vv. 4-18)

These verses tell us what God has done to save sinners. There are three great words in verses 4 and 5 — love, mercy and grace — and they all speak of an activity of God. It is God's love, God's mercy and God's grace that bring salvation to lost sinners. That is why Paul says in verse 10 that a Christian is God's workmanship. He means that believers are the product of the activity of God.

Out of God's love and mercy flows grace, and grace is not some abstract idea. It is God working. Grace is God loving the unlovely, pardoning the guilty and saving the lost. Grace is the unique work of God. We do not deserve grace, because our sin is our own fault. What we deserve is hell, but in Christ we receive grace and every blessing and benefit that flows from it. It is amazing that people want to believe in a salvation accomplished by their own efforts when God is freely offering us grace. Who wants their own pathetic efforts when we can have God's perfect salvation?

Because salvation is by grace it is perfect. By that we mean that God saves in such a way that we can never be lost again. Notice in verse 7 how Paul is talking of 'the coming ages'. Salvation by grace is an eternal salvation. It depends upon the merit of Christ, not our merit; therefore it never fails or loses its power.

How can we receive grace? Through faith, says verse 8. Bear in mind that Paul goes on to stress in verse 9 that salvation is not of works, not the result of our own efforts. So faith is not some good thing we do. It is a gift of God. Faith is not some vague optimism and certainly not an empty self-confidence. Faith looks towards what God has done. It looks at the cross in wonder and amazement and can hardly believe what it sees happening there. It asks,

Died he for me, who caused his pain?
For me, who him to death pursued?
Amazing love! How can it be
That thou, my God, shouldst die for me?

That is the language of faith as it throws itself upon the mercy and grace of God. The only reason for the existence of faith is the grace of God. The only thing worthy to put your faith in is the grace of God. Faith believes that what Jesus did in our place on the cross is enough to satisfy God. Faith believes God and calls upon Jesus to save the soul.

'Consequently...' (vv. 19-22)

Because of saving grace the repentant sinner is no longer what he was in verses 1-3. A great change has taken place and now he is a child of God. These verses describe what you can have in Christ. This is what we are saved to. We are saved *from* the power and consequence of sin and *to* the blessed privilege of knowing and enjoying God.

Qualified for heaven

We all understand the need for qualifications and we encourage our children to work hard at school and pass their exams because we know that without academic qualifications it will be difficult for them to obtain a good job. We accept this as a fact of life here and now in this world, but in today's reading Paul shows us that qualifications are also necessary with regard to the future life in heaven: 'giving thanks to the Father, who has qualified you to share in the inheritance of the saints in the kingdom of light' (v. 12).

In order to have a place in heaven we must have certain qualifications, but these are not intellectual or academic. They are not even moral or religious, and they are certainly not qualifications that we can obtain by our own efforts. Only God the Father can make us qualified. How does he do this? In order for a person to be qualified for heaven two things are necessary: his sin must be dealt with and his position or standing before God changed.

Sin must be dealt with (v. 14)

Man's natural condition is one of slavery to sin. Spiritually speaking, man is anything but free. The chains which bind him are not made of steel but of something far stronger. They are the chains of a depraved nature which finds submission to God impossible, chains of a deluded mind which thinks it is free and cannot see its true condition.

Redemption is the act by which God sets sinners free. It means deliverance by means of the payment of a ransom price. The New Testament tells us over and over again that the ransom price is the blood of Christ (1 Peter 1:18-19). The word 'blood' points, as it always does in the New Testament, to the sacrificial death of Jesus on the cross. As we have seen, by his death Jesus paid the debt our sin owed to God's holy law for all the violations of that law which we had committed. Jesus paid the debt in full and as a result of that payment there is for sinners a full and free pardon. It is this, and this alone, that qualifies us for heaven.

Our standing before God changed (v. 13)

Part of the purpose of the saving grace of God is to take the sinner out of the kingdom of spiritual darkness and to put him into the kingdom of the Son of God. This act of grace changes our standing before God: instead of being enemies we become children and as children of God we are qualified for heaven.

Notice how Paul uses the word 'rescued' to describe this action of God. For the meaning of this word see the illustrations in the chapter at the end of the book called 'Rescued'.

The rescued sinner becomes a citizen of a new kingdom and the moment he is saved he becomes a citizen of heaven. He is qualified immediately for heaven. Heaven is guaranteed from that moment. The Bible also describes salvation as becoming a member of the family of God, a joint heir with Christ of all the riches of God. How would you like to be adopted by a millionaire? Think of all the possibilities — no more money worries etc. It is not very likely to happen but there is something far better that is a distinct possibility — adoption by God. Think of all that would mean— acceptance by God, all your sins forgiven and a guaranteed place in heaven.

This is what redemption gives the sinner. Are you redeemed? How did the Colossians to whom Paul was writing obtain redemption?

First of all, they heard the gospel (vv. 5-6). You have heard it in this book. What are you going to do with this gospel?

There is only one sensible thing to do: believe it and turn to God in repentance and faith. Ask him to rescue you and thus to qualify you for an eternity in heaven.

A personal testimony

Today we see the apostle Matthew providing for us a personal testimony of how he became a follower of Christ. How an individual comes to faith is a very personal and precious thing. It is a once-in-a-lifetime experience, unrepeatable and unquestionably the most important and influential event that can happen to a person.

As Matthew puts before us this piece of autobiography the simplicity of the event is striking. We have a tendency to make conversion complicated and involved when in fact it all boils down to Jesus saying, 'Follow me,' and the sinner obeying that call. Though it is simple it is none the less a miracle of grace. Notice what precedes Matthew's call by Christ. In verses 1-8 he tells us of a healing miracle and then it is as if the apostle says, 'I will tell them next of another miracle, a greater one of how a man dead in sin was forgiven and given new life.' Every conversion of a sinner to Christ is a miracle, a wonder of grace. Only God could do it; therefore there is hope for all. If Matthew could be saved then so can you.

So stop reading for a moment and pray to the Lord who has been dealing with your soul as you have read this book, that he will call you to himself as he did Matthew.

Matthew was a tax collector. This was generally regarded as a job for thieves and dishonest men because it was open to all sorts of abuse. So when we read in verse 9 that Jesus saw him, he really saw him — saw his heart and life. Nothing was hidden from the Saviour. He saw a heart deep in sin. He saw every devious trick that Matthew had ever pulled. Jesus saw a man immune to God and not interested in faith and religion. When Jesus saw Matthew he saw him as he was, yet he still loved him and said, 'Follow me.'

Doesn't that give you hope? We have seen God being interested in and loving respectable, religious people, like Cornelius, but here in this tax collector is a man the exact opposite to Cornelius. Your sin is no barrier to your becoming a Christian. Jesus says in verse 13, 'For I have not come to call the righteous, but sinners.' The grace of God is stronger than your sin.

Jesus spoke to Matthew. He told him, he commanded him, 'Follow me.' Every conversion will have in it elements particular to the individual but all conversions have this in common: Jesus calls sinners to come to him. Christ still speaks by his Holy Spirit through his Word. Today he does not speak audibly, as he did to Matthew, but to the heart and mind and the conscience. He convicts of sin and shows us our need of him. Why are you reading a book like this when perhaps a year or so ago it would have been the last type of book to have interested you? Isn't Jesus speaking to you?

If the Saviour is speaking he is saying, 'Follow me: leave your sin, repent, come to me for pardon and new life.' How will you respond to such a call? Matthew simply got up and followed Jesus and that is what you need to do. Do you want to become a Christian? Are you serious about this? Do you see salvation as the most important thing in life? If you do, then Christ is already speaking to you.

Faith comes from hearing and you have heard. If you believe what God has been saying in the Scriptures we have looked at, then do something about it. Do the only thing you can do: turn in prayer now to God, confess your sin, thank him for what Christ has done for you and ask for salvation.

Rescued!

In 1976 an airliner with 244 passengers aboard was hijacked by Arab terrorists. It was then flown to Entebbe in Uganda where the Jewish passengers were separated from the rest and threatened with death if the Israeli government did not meet the terrorists' demands.

Israel decided to rescue its people. With great secrecy a rescue plan was devised. The need for secrecy was clear: the enemy must not know of the rescue plans or they would thwart them.

God did it differently. When he decided to rescue his people held captive in sin by the one whom Jesus called 'the strong man armed', he told everyone. Thousands of years before the event he said that the seed of a woman would be the rescuer. Then over the years God announced that the same rescuer would be of the family of David and born in Bethlehem. He even gave details of the rescue plan in many Old Testament passages.

Why did he did he do this? There are several reasons that we do not need to go into now, but did it not demonstrate the confidence God had in his Rescuer and the rescue plan?

Then when the Rescuer came into the world God sent a choir of angels to announce it and put a special star in the sky to proclaim it. And the rescue was not by plane-loads of heavily armed commandos, but a baby.

The devil must have thought that his task was easy. All that he had to do was to kill the baby, but even baby Jesus was too much for Satan.

Nothing happened for thirty years after this birth but Satan must surely have kept an eye on Nazareth. No doubt he told his spies to keep him in touch and to let him know at once if the Rescuer tried anything.

Then Jesus began to preach and heal the sick. Alarm bells rang in hell. 'Red alert!' cried Satan, 'The rescue is on!' To stop Jesus was now his sole intention. The temptations in the wilderness were part of Satan's plan to frustrate the rescue plan. Then eventually Satan entered into Judas and Jesus was betrayed.

Kill Jesus. Crucify him — Satan no doubt thought that was the end of God's rescue plan. Foolish Satan!

Death could not hold its prey,
He tore the bars away.
Up from the grave he arose,
With a mighty triumph o'er his foes.

For centuries 'the strong man armed' had kept his goods in peace but now a stronger than he had come (Luke 11:21-22).

Jesus rescued his people. He paid the debt they owed. He broke the power of sin in their lives. He destroyed the works of the devil.

Are you rescued? Are you saved?

A few years ago I was on holiday at a seaside resort and we saw a rescue in action. The engine of a fishing boat out [...] down and it was drifting onto the [...] e saw two red flares coming from [...] y had seen their plight and the [...] ad no power and could do nothing [...] flares said, 'Come and rescue us.' [...] sped across the bay towards the [...] They threw rescue lines to her and [...] rocks and then towed her to the [...]

[...]ed? You need rescuing. Your sin [...] on the rocks of divine justice. [...] n do to save yourself, so send up [...] y to rescue you.

[...] us Christ and be saved.

Other titles by the same author

Books especially helpful for new and young Christians

All things new
A help for those beginning the Christian life.

Christian handbook
A straightforward guide to the Bible, church history and Christian doctrine.

Firm foundations
A two-month daily reading course in some great chapters of the Bible.

*Great God of wonders**
The attributes of God.

Stand firm
A young Christian's guide to the armour of God.

Stepping stones
A guide for beginners to the books of the New Testament.

Walk worthy
Guidelines for those beginning the Christian life.

Other titles

How to behave in church*
A guide to church life based on studies in 1 Timothy.

I will never become a Christian
Some of the reasons people give for not becoming Christians.

Our present suffering
Why Christians experience sickness and suffering and how they should face such trials.

Seeking God
For those who are earnestly seeking God.

Sickness and death in the Christian family*
Examples from the Bible of how the Christian faces sickness and bereavement.

Struggling but winning*
A survival guide for Christians based on the experiences of Old Testament characters.

Religion to Christ
The new birth explained from John 3.

Windows of truth
Illustrations on the way of salvation and the Christian life.

The Young Spurgeon*
The story of the early years of this famous preacher, based on his own account.

*Also published by Evangelical Press